a Color Game

retold by Ruby Mae ● illustrated by John Steven Gurney

HARCOURT BRACE & COMPANY

Orlando Atlanta Austin Boston San Francisco Chicago Dallas New York
Toronto London

Green, green, green
is everything I'm wearing.
Green, green, green is everything I own.
I have chosen green to be my color
for I chose this green tree for my home.

Blue, blue, blue
is everything I'm wearing.
Blue, blue, blue is everything I own.
I have chosen blue to be my color
for I chose the blue sky in my room.

Yellow, yellow, yellow
is everything I'm wearing.
Yellow, yellow, yellow is everything I own.
I have chosen yellow to be my color
for I chose the yellow sun to shine.

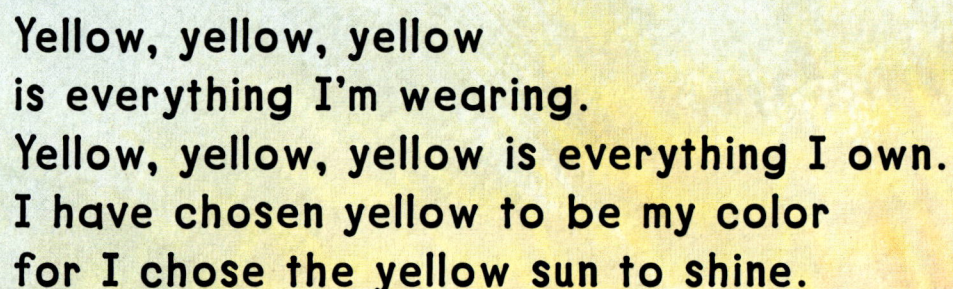

Red, red, red
is everything I'm wearing.
Red, red, red is everything I own.
I have chosen red to be my color
for I chose a red dog to be my pet.

Purple, purple, purple
is everything I'm wearing.
Purple, purple, purple is everything I own.
I have chosen purple to be my color
for I chose a purple kite to fly up high.

Brown, brown, brown
is everything I'm wearing.
Brown, brown, brown is everything I own.
I have chosen brown to be my color
for I chose the brown mud to play in.

White, white, white
is everything I'm wearing.
White, white, white is everything I own.
I have chosen white to be my color
for I chose the white clouds to sleep on.